The Heart of Transformation

And The Butterfly Effect

Verlaine Crawford

High Castle Publishing

THE HEART OF TRANSFORMATION
AND THE BUTTERFLY EFFECT

Copyright © 2020 by Verlaine Crawford. All rights reserved.
Printed and Published in the United States by High Castle Publishing

Print Version ISBN-13: 978-0-9998036-3-9
E-Book ISBN-13: 978-0-9998036-4-6

This is a work of non-fiction. No part of this book may be used or reproduced in any manner without written permission except in the case of brief quotations embodied in critical articles and reviews.

Front Cover Photo of Butterfly by David Mark from Pixabay.
Back Cover Photo of Butterfly & Rose by Hans Benn from Pixabay.
Cover and Interior Design by Verlaine Crawford.

1. Personal Growth & Development 2. Self-Help. 3. Inspirational
4. Spiritual Growth 5. Visionary & Metaphysical. 6. Harmony Within
7. Body, Mind, and Spirit. 8. Health and Well-Being.
9. New Thought 10. Psychology

I. Title

First Edition

This Book is dedicated to...

All those who have viewed the sky

with wonder and wished

that they could fly.

Table of Contents

Preface

Who Are You?

Each Day is the First Day of the Rest of Your Life

The Butterfly Effect

If We Are Fragmented, How Did It Happen?

Transformation!

Are We a Blank Slate at Birth?

The Power of the Heart

Are Your Beliefs Serving You?

What Is A Belief?

Becoming Aware of the Many Parts of You

Life is a Biofeedback System

The People Around You Are Different Parts of You

Becoming "My Angel"

Is There a Way to Bring All Your Opposing Parts Together?

What is the Infusion Integration Technique?

Using the Infusion Integration Technique

Cosmic Bridges and the Desires of Your Heart

Moment Points, Magnetic Fields, and Manifestation

A Note from Verlaine

About the Author

Order Books by Verlaine Crawford

Preface

It was a very hot, humid day on the Island of Bali. The ocean waves were twinkling like diamonds as the sun cast its light on the beautiful bay, highlighted the sandy beach, and filtered through the tall palm trees overhead. I was there as a speaker and participant for an Earth Day Conference, sponsored by Power Places Tours.

One of the presenters was describing the meditation she was about to direct. She explained that during the meditation, she would ring the small, Tibetan Bells she held in her hands. The first ringing would lift our consciousness from the base chakra ("survival" at the root of the spine) to the second chakra ("creativity" at the level of the belly button). The next ringing would move our consciousness to the third chakra (our "power center" at the solar plexus) and then to the fourth chakra to our hearts (the energy of Love and the source of creation).

At the fifth ringing of the bells, we would move our awareness to our throats (our communication center) and the sixth to the third eye (intuition) followed by the seventh to the crown chakra (our spiritual connection). At the eighth ring, our consciousness would rise above our heads to the angelic realm; and finally, at the ninth ringing, we would move higher still into the flow of Universal Consciousness.

I relaxed, sitting cross-legged on a blanket spread on the grass under the trees, closed my eyes, and followed her directions as she rang the bells. At the sound of the last ringing, I found myself floating among the stars. The feeling and sensations were of expansive freedom beyond anything I could have imagined. There were no boundaries. I was in space and space was in me. There were no questions to ask and no fear or confusion.

I was just floating among the stars when I heard a voice pleading, "Verlaine come back! Verlaine come back!" Friends sitting near me noticed that I was turning blue. They became afraid and were calling out to me.

I heard the voices and wondered, "What is a Verlaine?" I had no idea about an earthly body or even the earth.

They were pleading louder, "Verlaine come back!"

Just then, I heard a phrase in my mind: "A name is a word with memories attached."

"Oh, yes," I thought, "That word must be my name. They are calling me. There must be memories attached to that name. Gradually, I moved back into my body and opened my eyes to the immense relief of the people gathered around me.

As my consciousness settled back into my body, it was interesting to see so much light around my friends and an effervescent glow around the plants, flowers, and trees. Everything was emitting multicolored, pastel colors like soft clouds of iridescent light.

It took days to integrate the expansive energy I had experienced. When I was around people, I felt as if there was a balloon of light surrounding me that moved in and out every time I came near another person.

The effects of that moment still echo through my days. My journey among the stars has changed my perspective on being present in this lifetime. The memory and feeling of that experience are always with me. I know we are all One with the Universe.

"*Universe*" is an interesting word. It can be divided into Uni = Unified. And Verse, which is defined as a single metrical line in a poetic composition, one line of poetry, or a song. We are each a part of the poetry…we are each a part of the unified song of the Cosmos.

This was one of many experiences I have lived that made me aware of the realm beyond the physical, mental, and emotional world that we normally inhabit. I have had the opportunity to test and trust my intuitive guidance, which has always led me to my highest good.

This is the first in a proposed series of books in which I will discuss my understanding of many aspects of life, including health, wealth, love, self-expression, and spiritual awakening.

I desire to share what I have learned and provide my evidence and experience of a Higher Conscious awareness that is available to each of us during every moment of our lives on Earth and beyond.

Chapter 1

Who Are You?

You are far greater than you mind,
your body, and emotions.
You are a Being of Light
manifesting in human form.

You were born into this world capable of learning about the beauty of nature, the facility of languages, the intimacy of relationships, the unfolding of history, the mysteries of science, the dynamics of mathematics, and so much more.

You were an empty computer filled with love and equipped with a myriad of emotions that would allow you to participate in the excitement and drama of being alive on a beautiful planet. Arriving in the world, you were full of energy, curiosity, and enthusiasm, destined to become the very best person you could be.

And then the programming began. If you were fortunate, you had loving, responsible, and dedicated parents to help you learn about your talents and abilities.

Unfortunately, most people were raised by parents who were too busy to do parenting. They were great at saying, "No!" when you wanted to explore new places or ideas. They imposed their version of how you should *act* and what you should *do* regardless of whether their plans matched the incredibly amazing human you were capable of being.

Even if your caretakers were encouraging and helpful, you were still confronted by thousands of voices, millions of words, and pictures that programmed you with conflicting beliefs. Your mind eventually consisted of bits and pieces of an enormous jigsaw puzzle of concepts and ideas that rarely fit together in a cohesive form.

Becoming Fractured

Many people on the planet have become fractured by a myriad of competing voices. Parents, friends, teachers, politicians, religious leaders, professionals, actors, media hosts, authors, movie producers, and more propagate their ideas about every possible subject.

These competing concepts coming from all directions cause confusion and emotional upheaval. The deluge of personal opinions framed as facts eventually fractures the brain's organizing principle of rational thinking.

Years of cross-referencing, victimizing, blaming, and hateful commentary eliminate the central core of a peaceful mind. Caught in a web of chaos, the individual weakens. The spark of life dims, and the power and will to succeed often fade and evaporate into the confusion called life.

Exhausted by a mind constantly attacking internally and flipping from one subject to another, individuals give up control of their lives and follow the path of least resistance. They end up with voices in their heads telling them to do this or that, arguing with them, denigrating their spirits, dampening their enthusiasm, and eliminating their ability to expand and truly enjoy life.

This book, "The Heart of Transformation" is meant to give you answers about how to work with all those voices inside your head by imagining them to be sub-personalities. You will be able to reason with those parts-of-you and integrate them into the whole of your being.

The premise of sharing this information from my heart to your heart is for you to be able to expand your inner strength and power to create a peaceful, harmonious place in which to dwell. You must have the ability to wipe away false perceptions and see the world more clearly and joyfully.

Hopefully, with this information and by using the Infusion Integration Technique, you will gain the wisdom and understanding to make informed decisions easily. You will be able to relax into success, health, creativity, and to love yourself and others and your life completely.

Chapter 2

Each Day is the First Day
of The Rest of Your Life

*We Think of Ourselves
as Captain of Our Ship...
Master of Our Fate.
But I See It as a Pirate Ship,
and the Crew is Planning Mutiny.*

Yes, you have the power at this moment to pursue your passion. You can guide your ship to new lands of plenty, follow your Spiritual Guidance to marvelous experiences, and you can change your mind to change your course of action throughout your life.

You are a creator. You are the keeper of beliefs that form thoughts. Those thoughts combined with emotions activate feelings that influence your decisions to act. The energy of those decisions leads to actions that create your reality.

Over the years, you have gathered and memorized information from family members, friends, school, work associates, the media, and more. You piece together your version of reality based on a huge variety of statements that you have adopted as truth. Those statements are like seeds planted in your sub-conscious. They can be life-affirming or life stopping ideas that influence every aspect of your thinking and thus your actions. The results of those actions or inactions become your life.

But is your version of reality true? Is it real?

Look at your life. Who are you? What is your Soul purpose? Why are you here on Planet Earth?

Look again...go deeper...delve into the center and journey into your essence. This is the time for you to become all you came to be.

Chapter 3

The Butterfly Effect

*You become the cause that creates
an effect. Your transformation
reverberates to others around the world.*

I have always been fascinated by the amazing transformation of a caterpillar into a butterfly. It seems so outrageous that a little worm-like creature crawling over a tree limb can weave a cocoon and in less than thirty days, it will emerge as a beautiful, winged being flying gracefully through the air.

In chaos theory, it is said that we live in a system where every action produces a reaction…every cause creates an effect. Therefore, scientists explain *The Butterfly Effect* as a small change in one state (in your body, mind, spirit, nature, or the environment) that can result in larger changes in a later state.

Small changes can lead to huge differences in your life. When you go through a transformation, you accomplish more than changing your own life. Your thoughts and actions unleash transformational energy that produces a reaction in the people around you.

My understanding of how that could happen became even more important to me when I experienced one of the most difficult periods in my life.

It was 1987 and I was working on an exciting movie project in England and Wales about a psychic adventure story in which a family in Scotland went on a treasure hunt and discovered, "The Green Stone." I met the people who lived this amazing episode and had the pleasure to spend time with Robert Bolt, the script-writer for movies such as "Laurence of Arabia", "A Man for All Seasons", "Dr. Zhivago", "and Gandhi". Robert and his wife, the acclaimed actress, Sarah Miles, were interested in participating in the project.

After many amazing, other-worldly experiences in England and Wales, there came a time when it seemed that the Universe wanted me to stop, look, and listen to what was happening around me. There was no question that I was stopped.

I was in Los Angeles and went to see a movie starring an actress who could play the lead in the project. We arrived late and the movie was already playing.

As I climbed the stairs in the theater, I turned to see if my mother and friends were following me. Mom seemed to be having a difficult time climbing the stairs, so I decided to go down and help her. At that moment the movie changed to a night scene. The theater went dark. There were no lights on the stairs. I missed the step and fell headfirst down the steps, landing on my ribs with my foot twisted behind me.

The result was a broken foot and a rib and a lot of boring days ahead. Two weeks later I was tired of lying in bed and decided to attend a film festival in Beverly Hills, and after a full day on crutches, I became exhausted.

I was waiting for a friend to bring the car and moved too quickly. I lost my balance and fell backward off my crutches onto the curb and cracked my spine. My doctor who resembled my idea of a Zen master told me, "You are not to DO anything."

As I lay in my bed unable to move without pain and feeling like Humpty Dumpty, I began to think about the Butterfly. "How does the caterpillar transform?" I wondered. "What happens to that little crawling worm in its womb-like cocoon? Does it feel broken as it begins to transform?"

I asked my Mom to bring me a book about butterflies. (This was 1987 before we could look up everything on Google.) She brought me a children's book about a butterfly.

In the story, as the caterpillar was eating its dinner, it became aware that a change was coming. She could feel it in every fiber of her being. She waited. The days went by slowly. And then one day, she knew it was time to transform.

Somehow the caterpillar knew how to wind herself into a cocoon hanging from a limb of a tree. She was wrapped snuggly and then relaxed. After a while, her body started to move without her volition. She felt the rhythm of an internal dance and became the witness, watching herself beginning to change in her tightly wound cocoon.

Time passed and nothing seemed to happen. Suddenly, without warning, the caterpillar felt an explosion. It was as if all parts of her being were blown into pieces—tiny fragments of energy that looked like starlight surrounded her body.

She gasped as the fragments began to take form. Curved designs appeared to her right and left, feelers and legs and even a tail were vibrating around the central core of her being. She watched, waited, and felt the energy solidify as wings began to form. They looked like patterns of energy vibrating close to her body.

Eventually, it was time to move through the walls of the cocoon and become free to fly high into the sky. She would no longer be crawling cautiously upon the branches. She was renewed and changed. She was transformed.

Why do we need to transform to become who we wish to be?

In you, me, the human race…our psyches are fragmented. We live in a confused state of opposing beliefs, experiencing a battle within ourselves that reveals itself with conflicting voices requesting changes. Those inner voices are demanding that we stick to a routine and fulfill our responsibilities, or they are crying out for the freedom to make spontaneous choices. They might want to quit your job and follow a new career or lay on the beach and soak up the sun.

It is as if parts of us have never grown up. They have been isolated in their little world simply holding onto their version of reality, trying to get their wants and desires. They can interrupt our progress and demand attention. If we don't give them what they want, they try to stop us with an illness, develop problems at work, arguments with the family, and or create a fuzzy mind that can't concentrate effectively.

These alienated parts-of-us are trying to help us, but we don't listen to what they are saying. We don't acknowledge what they are trying to accomplish.

We hear opposing concepts arguing in our heads:

Responsible Self: "Hurry up and get to work."
Opposition: "I want to go to the beach. Why am I going to work?
Responsible: "I need the money."
Opposition: "Why can't I have fun?"
Responsible: "What is fun?"

Healthy Self: "Let's go for a walk."
Workaholic Self: "I don't have time to waste."
Healthy Self: "But you have been sitting there at the computer for 5 hours."
Workaholic Self: "I have to get this done."

Healthy Self: "But you keep making mistakes because you are tired and need to move around."

Workaholic Self: "Leave me alone! Shut up about the walk already!"

Chapter 4

If We Are Fragmented, How Did It Happen?

Caught in the windmill of my mind,
my truth and identity I cannot find.

We become fragmented as our minds absorb a huge amount of conflicting information. We are constantly bombarded by a variety of concepts, ideas, and beliefs, which become part of us through the experiences we have lived, heard, read about, and witnessed. Usually, we don't question the information. It simply goes into our memory (our subconscious) unfiltered.

As the years go by, each of us gathers thousands of concepts about the world. These concepts become beliefs. Once the ideas and observations we have absorbed become beliefs, the concepts are no longer questioned.

An example would be: A little girl learns that boys can be mean and rough. At the same time, she learns that boys can be cute and sweet. She catalogs two opposing beliefs, and eventually, the proof for each pattern of beliefs begins to accumulate. The girl files away two separate beliefs about boys and later may add more opposing beliefs about men.

Whether the beliefs are productive/energizing, or destructive/depressive, opposing beliefs stop us from achieving our goals. These inner conflicts cause stress that undermines our health, caps our wealth, disrupts our relationships, and stifles our ability to be creative, adventurous, and full of life!

We become fragmented and essentially less able to handle new activities and events, accidents and upsets, frustration, and confusion. We live in a battle within ourselves and thus, the battle shows up outside of ourselves, reflecting our thoughts, actions, and behaviors.

Chapter 5

Transformation!

I am alive and well and fully aligned.
I am a new being who is no longer blind.

Are you ready for a change, a shift in consciousness that lifts you into another dimension filled with the excitement of a well-lived life?

Are you willing to move into the chrysalis and allow your mind, body, and spirit to be transformed into an agent of change so that you can truly fly?

Transformation!
What a dynamic word: Trans...form...ation.

The combination of syllables in the word *transformation* seems to *flow and move*. The *sound of the word* creates atonality, a ringing forth, describing a new way of seeing, feeling, and being.

The prefix: 'trans' comes from Latin and means "across," "beyond," "through," "changing thoroughly". Transforming is always active, forever inventive, creative, and unending.

Our bodies are constantly transforming. New cells are replacing the trillions of old cells in our skin, organs, and bones every moment of the day. Our physical body is made up of a process of chemicals, water, and electrical energy constantly moving around and through our bodies.

Our minds are transforming as we learn new skills, absorb information, and utilize our talents and abilities. Music, theater, books, art and design, natural environments, mathematics and science, religious experiences, and spiritual awakening can help our minds to transform as we become inspired and begin to grasp new concepts and ideas.

We each can transform our hearts and minds, our physical bodies, and our environment. We can transform and enliven our focus, goals, and commitments. Transformation is a renewal of our ability to live fully and to feel the energy of excitement.

I desire to help you learn the Heart of Transformation, so that you may become all that you can be.

Chapter 6

Are We a Blank Slate at Birth?

*Am I a soul that travels through time
or an empty computer so sweet and sublime?*

There is a concept that humans are born into this world innocent and without knowledge or information. We are considered to be a blank slate that is written upon by others, and we absorb information through language and experiences. This appears to be true as we watch the child become programmed with a myriad of ideas and concepts while we learn about nature, humans, and other life forms.

Some people on the planet believe that we come in as a baby with knowledge from previous lives. Others conjecture that our DNA holds talents and perhaps memories of our ancestors.

Regardless of who is correct, by the time we are three years old if not earlier, our distinct personalities are quite apparent. Our talents, abilities, and our ways of acting and reacting to the world and other people seem to be quite developed and distinct from our siblings (even in the case of identical twins), our parents, and other children.

From birth, we begin the process of receiving thoughts and beliefs that form the filter through which we see the world around us. This process creates an ego and a concept of who we are and what we can and cannot do

Who Are You?

You are energy in form. Look through an electron microscope, and you will see the cells of your body at the level of atoms. Atoms are made up of three particles: protons, neutrons, and electrons. Those particles are spinning around a nucleus within an enormous area of open space within the atom.

You are not solid, you are composed of energetic particles held within atoms. Those atoms are forming and reforming the cells of organs, nerves, brain matter, skin, and the structure of your body and mind.

You are the light essence manifesting as a human being.

You are a grand and outrageous Human Being, which can be translated as:

Hue = color = vibrational frequency of light
Man = manifesting
Being = present in the Now

You are a vibrational frequency of light manifesting in the present…in the Now.

You are a holographic image of the universe, mirroring the splendor and magnificence of creation. Your essence is Universal Consciousness, the Spirit of the Creator, manifesting in the energetic form that we call physicality.

You are composed of layers of energy vibrating at different frequencies.

Your Spiritual body, which is your *Over-Soul*, vibrates with the etheric energy known as the Celestial Realm. It is the lightest, quickest moving energy of your energetic structure. This *Over-Soul* forms an aura, which appears as a transparent envelope of energy around your mental, emotional, and physical bodies. This is the energy beyond your mind. It is often called your "Intuition", inner knowing, which vibrates at the level of the Celestial Realm, the 6th Dimension.

Your Mental Body is a very fast-moving energetic level holding all your thoughts and concepts. This is called the Causal Plane since thought creates your reality. (This is known as the Mental Realm, the 5th Dimension.)

Your Emotional Body is denser and affects the physical body directly. It is the energy of your ever-fluctuating emotions. It is where thoughts combine with the energy of emotion—energy in motion—and thus activate your mental creation into form. (This is the Astral Realm, the 4th Dimension.)

Your Physical Body is the densest, slowest moving level of energy that acts as the structure formed by your thoughts and emotions (This is the 3rd Dimensional reality of everything physical on the planet).

Energy Wheels – the Chakras

Within your energetic fields are energy wheels, called chakras that correspond to the glands of the body. The varying fields of energy move through the body in a double helix pattern and move around the body like a rainbow of light.

7 - (Violet) Crown Chakra is Spirituality – I Am

6 - (Indigo) Third Eye is Intuition/Awareness – I know

5 - (Blue) Throat is Communication – I think/speak

4 - (Green) Heart is Love – The Center of Spiritual Power

3 - (Gold) Solar Plexus – Worldly Power

2 - (Orange) Sacral Chakra – Creativity and Sexual Energy

1 - (Red) Root Chakra – Survival, Trust, and Fear

The Heart is the Center of the Your Energy System.

Chapter 7

The Power of the Heart

*When you are in alignment
spiritually, mentally, emotionally, and physically,
you reflect the pure essence of your true self.
You radiate love, creativity,
harmony, expansion, and joy.*

Why is the title of this book "The *Heart* of Transformation"? What is so important about the heart in our transformational process? It has become apparent that the heart is not only the center of our Chakra System, but the heart-mind connection is also a major element in our understanding of the world and the intuition, thoughts, and emotions we use as our guidance system.

Over the past twenty years, the scientists at *HeartMath Institute* have been studying the electrical and magnetic fields around the heart. They have discovered that the heart is about 100 times stronger electrically and 5000 times stronger magnetically than the brain. The electromagnetic field of your heart can be measured up to a few feet away from your body.

It is interesting to consider the heart as another brain. In addition to generating the strongest electromagnetic field, the heart appears to have an intelligence of its own, which is why some neuro-cardiologists refer to it as the heart-brain or the fifth brain.

Scientists have learned that the nervous system of the heart contains roughly 40,000 neurons or sensory neurites, which monitor the heart's hormones, neurochemicals, heart rate, and blood pressure information. This information about the state of these chemicals is sent to the brain.

The heart and brain are always communicating through the *vagus* nerve, which is one of the cranial nerves that connect the brainstem to the body. This nerve has two bunches of sensory nerve cells that allow the brain to monitor and receive information about the body's different functions

It is through this dynamic communication process that the *consciousness* of the heart can change how the brain processes information. This process can also affect how energy flows in the body.

The heart works with the brain and body, including the amygdala. Normally, there are two amygdalae per person, with one amygdala on each side of the brain. They are thought to be a part of the limbic system within the brain, which is responsible for emotions, survival instincts, and memory.

The amygdala helps us make decisions about incoming information and processes that information based on our past experiences. The heart filters information to be sent to the brain, which affects our perception of the world around us.

Therefore, the heart/mind/body and Spiritual connection all work together to help us become whole and true to ourselves.

I believe that what we call our Soul is our *Over-Soul* Consciousness anchored in our hearts. That Soul energy is part of the egg-like energy pattern that surrounds our body and moves through the energy centers of the Chakras and the other acupuncture points in our Meridians. (In acupuncture and Chinese medicine meridians are of a set of pathways in the body through which vital energy flows. There are twelve such pathways associated with specific organs.)

If we follow our hearts, we are listening to the subtle voice of intuition and Spiritual Guidance. In Eastern Spiritual Tradition, when people speak of the mind, they point to their hearts. Therefore, *Mindfulness* would be *Heartfulness*!

Chapter 8

Are Your Beliefs Serving You?

As the oak tree begins as a tiny seed,
your beliefs are the seeds that create your deeds.

Are the concepts and beliefs you have gathered over your lifetime now serving you in your health, wealth, relationships, and creative expression? Are you living your life in alignment with your Soul Essence?

In 1994, I published a book called, "Ending the Battle Within: How to Create a Harmonious Life Working with Your Sub-Personalities." The concept of "Ending the Battle Within" was to help people understand that each of us has many parts-of-our-being. Those sub-personalities are holding a variety of concepts and ideas that are solidified into beliefs. Many of those beliefs serve you well. Other beliefs are in direct opposition to your heart's desires.

The Keepers of Your Beliefs

Either way, the parts of you who are holding those positive or negative beliefs always think they are helping you. Strange but true. After working with thousands of people, I have learned that the part-of-you who is stopping you from moving forward in your life always think they are helping and/or protecting you in some way.

Those beliefs may be misinformed, but parts of you are holding onto beliefs that stop your progress and limit your manifestation because they think they are helping you by causing problems in your life. It is very important to find out what those *Keepers of Your Beliefs* think. What are the advantages of ill health, upsetting relationships, lack of money, and loss of creative expression in your life?

I am presenting this information as a quick guide that you can use to neutralize "The Battle Within". You can learn to do the Infusion Integration Technique and experience your full power through WHOLENESS.

Chapter 9

What is a Belief?

Beliefs are patterns of words, a statement
that set the stage for the play,
which becomes your drama unfolding each day.

The word "Belief" is defined as 'personal attitudes associated with ideas and concepts." I consider a "Belief" to be any group of words we put together into a sentence that defines an idea or concept and we accept that statement as our truth.

Often the sentences we consider to be true have been passed down through the generations as folk wisdom or religious teachings to be shared.

Benjamin Franklin, inventor, philosopher, scientist, and statesman was one of the purveyors of such wisdom:

"Early to bed and early to rise makes a man healthy, wealthy, and wise."

"God helps those who help themselves."

"An investment in knowledge pays the best interest."

"When you are finished changing, you are finished."

"They who can give up essential liberty to obtain temporary safety deserve neither liberty nor safety."

Statements that came from:

Confucius, the Chinese philosopher, teacher, and political leader:
"Wheresoever you go, go with all your heart."

"He who knows all the answers has not been asked all the questions."

"Study the past if you would define the future."

"Respect yourself and others will respect you."

"I hear and I forget. I see and I remember.
I do and I understand."

Christian Faith:
"So I say to you, ask and it will be given to you; search, and you will find; knock, and the door will be opened for you."

"For what shall it profit a man, if he gains the whole world and suffers the loss of his soul?"

"Teacher, which commandment is the greatest in the Law?" Jesus declared, "Love the Lord your God with all your heart and with all your soul and with all your mind."

"Seek ye first the kingdom of Heaven and all else will be added unto you."

Buddhist Faith:
"Just as a candle cannot burn without fire, men cannot live without a spiritual life."

"A man is not called wise because he talks and talks again; but if he is peaceful, loving, and fearless then he is in truth called wise."

"If the problem can be solved why worry? If the problem cannot be solved worrying will do you no good."

"It is a man's own mind, not his enemy or foe that lures him to evil ways."

"The Way is not in the sky; the Way is in the heart."

And statements that became beliefs from my mother, Elaine:

"Never go anywhere empty-handed.
(When cleaning the house.).

"Don't go out in the rain. You will catch a cold."

"Accomplish all your chores before you have fun."

"What's worth doing is worth doing well."

"You can do anything!"

Each statement is a series of words strung together in a sentence. Those sentences are stored as thoughts that become beliefs. We all have thousands of concepts that we consider to be truths. Thousands of sentences are helpful, some are detrimental. And there are many beliefs, which conflict with each other.

Statements in Conflict

Being rich would be great. I could help so many people. I could build hospitals and schools. I could share my wealth and travel around the world.

Versus

The rich are never happy. They have to pay a lot of taxes. They are greedy, and remember from the Bible, "It is easier for a camel to go through the eye of a needle than for a rich person to enter the Kingdom of God!"

If you believe strongly in the second group of sentences, you undoubtedly will have difficulty receiving more than enough money let alone wealth in your life.

Random Sentences Become Your Beliefs.

Your beliefs, known as truths, serve as the basis of your thoughts. As we have mentioned, they are the seed from which your thoughts arise. You would not plant tomato seeds and expect an orange tree to grow. Therefore, what is planted in your sub-conscious is destined to appear in your life.

When those thoughts are activated by emotion (energy in motion), they become catalysts for your decisions and actions that create your reality…the life you are experiencing today.

How Do You Know What You Believe?

Look carefully at your life. Your life gives you clues to what you believe. Life is the manifestation of your beliefs.

Why would anyone believe a life of struggle is normal? Because people and media programmed them to believe that it is normal to have problems, sacrifices, ill health, and upsetting relationships. It is important to ask these questions:

What were the thoughts that manifested the life I have now? What did I believe and why?

What type of home, health, wealth, auto, job, relationships, creative expression, and fun do I have?

Is my current life full of opportunity?

Am I experiencing abundance?

Do I give and receive love?

Am I healthy and vibrant?

Do I feel happy and joyfully alive?

Do I express myself creatively?

If you don't like the answers, it is time to transform.

Your beliefs and concepts can be changed. You can create the life of your dreams, but you need to know what you believe and how those beliefs are stopping you from receiving your heart's desires.

Chapter 10

Becoming Aware
of the Many Parts-Of-You

*You have many bit players within your being
who hold beliefs that may be demeaning and
always gathering data to support their meaning.*

Let's start with thinking in terms of your having many parts-of-you, many sub-personalities. If you think about who you are, you can easily determine that you probably have a distinct sub-personality for your workplace or school. You have another personality that you show when you are at home. There may be another persona when you are at a party or a sporting event, a fund-raiser, washing your car, or when you are traveling on vacation.

You even have different personalities that are apparent to family members, close friends, acquaintances, teachers, work associates, and a store clerk where you shop.

I like to think in terms of each of us harboring many *sub-personalities* who are the *Keepers of Our Beliefs.* It is the responsibility of each sub-personality to gather, maintain, and store proof and confirmation for their own particular set of beliefs.

One sub-personality may hold a positive, reinforcing belief, such as "I am very capable and talented." Another of your sub-personalities may believe, "I always seem to fail and nobody appreciates my talents."

As you might guess, this type of opposition can create inner discord. You might do very well at the beginning of a project, and then something will go wrong to fulfill the belief that you always fail.

Imagine your life in terms of a structure, a tall building that is set on four cornerstones—a strong base that serves as your grounding point of strength, endurance, and survival.

This base is your foundation, and I see it as…

The Four Cornerstones of Life

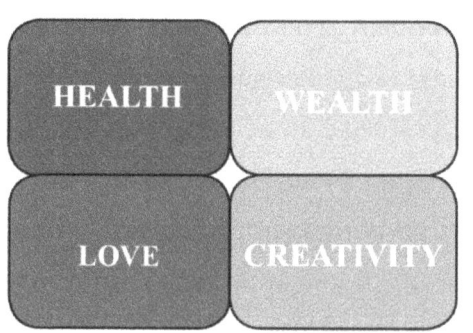

I any of the Four Cornerstones is missing the structure of your life begins to crumble.

It would be great if each of us only held positive beliefs about our health, wealth, loving relationships, and creative self-expression. Instead, we have been programmed with a myriad of beliefs through our interaction with others and exposure to the media. We become fractured into many personas and the job of those parts of us is to create as much proof as possible that those beliefs they are true.

It may be difficult for you to understand that all parts of you, all of your sub-personalities are holding onto *different* types of beliefs. Some hold positive beliefs that are helpful to your progress. Others hold what you might call negative beliefs that stop you from moving forward and making strengthening changes in your life.

I have found that even your negative sub-personalities think they are doing something *for* you. They always think they are helping you, protecting you, and keeping you safe in some way, even if they are making you sick, stopping you from receiving money, interrupting loving relationships, and preventing you from creatively fulfilling your purpose in life.

Once you understand what beliefs these sub-personalities are holding as truth, you can help them discover that there are other ways to handle whatever situation they are trying to control. You can help them understand that there is a broader belief that will allow you to succeed financially, improve your health, experience love, use your creativity, and protect you at the same time.

Very few people have examined their beliefs.

Even when we continue to meet negative people and upsetting experiences over and over again, we normally don't stop to reflect on what we believe. We have <u>not</u> been taught to examine our underlying beliefs about work, friendships and loving relationships, vibrant health, and fulfilling creative expression we want in our lives.

We need to review our underlying beliefs such as:

Is it better to be rich or poor or somewhere in between? What are your beliefs that support being rich? Perhaps they include the ability to travel, the ease with which you pay your bills and purchase new items, the freedom to work and play when you want to, etc.

Some beliefs support being poor such as the ability to be free of obligations, to live simply without many possessions, to ensure that no one will be jealous of you, and you don't need to pay high taxes.

The point is that if you have more beliefs that support not being rich, there is a good chance it will be more difficult to make money and gain wealth.

What is the key to understanding the parts-of-you that cling to concepts and beliefs that may be detrimental to your health, wealth, love, and self-expression?

All parts-of-you, no matter what they believe, whether it is seemingly good, bad, or upsetting, think they are *helping* you. Each sub-personality believes that they are doing something *FOR* you!

It is important to look closely at your beliefs and concepts that are creating your life.

What does a part of you believe are the advantages of not being healthy?

Examples: When I am sick…

- I can take it easy and rest.
- I have time to think about me.
- I don't have to go to work or school.
- Someone will take care of me.

What does a part of you believe the advantages are of not being wealthy?

Examples: Without wealth…

- I don't have to worry about investing.
- No one will love me just for my money.
- I can be free of responsibility.
- People won't be jealous of me.

What does a part of you believe the advantages are of being alone without a loving relationship?

Examples: Without a loving relationship…

- I can do what I want.
- I can be messy (or super neat).
- I don't have to worry about someone else.
- I won't be deserted by anyone.

What does a part of you believe the advantages are of not using your creative expression?

Examples: Without creative expression…

- Not a clue. I don't even know what that means.
- I follow my routine and get paid for my work.\
- I don't have to come up with new ideas or write a book or paint a painting.
- I don't have to worry that I am upsetting the applecart by introducing a new way of doing things.

When you understand how to work with your sub-personalities, you will be able to transform your life and create a unified energy field that develops and supports your strengths, talents, and abilities.

You will be able to find the answers and activate the techniques you need to reverse the beliefs that are holding you back. You will be able to create excellent health, abundant wealth, loving relationships, and life-enhancing creativity, AND you will also receive the benefits that the opposing beliefs were providing.

You will be able to use all your power to create a fulfilling life that you enjoy living.

Chapter 11

Life is a Biofeedback System

*Your life story is the result
of your thoughts and actions.*

It appears that life is a bio-feedback system. What you see is the result of what you believe. All the people and experiences that show up in your environment are the result of the concepts and beliefs that rule your life.

Life is co-creating evolution with us – meaning any belief, thought, or concept that we hold within ourselves that can be manifested is going to show up in a positive or negative experience in our waking dream, our "real" life.

If you look carefully at everything and everyone in your life, you may be able to trace back into your memory and discover when you had the thought or established a belief that brought you to the school you attend, the home where you live, the people in your life, and the work you have chosen.

Perhaps you imagined or considered it appropriate to live in an apartment or a 3 bedroom, 2 bath house or a mansion or perhaps aboard a sailboat, a yacht, or a cruise ship traveling around the world.

When you think a thought about what you would like in your life, it begins to move toward you. Perhaps you're thinking about owning a certain car or truck. You declare your desire to own such a vehicle. You imagine what it might feel like to drive it and visualize the way it would look in your driveway.

From that day forward, you probably begin to see many more of those particular cars or trucks on the road. Your mind will become magnetized to that vision, and you see it all around you. If you truly desire this vehicle, perhaps you begin saving money, you see an advertisement that the car you want is available at a good price, or sometimes it happens that someone loans you that vehicle or perhaps even gives it to you. Your thought combined with a caring emotion magnetizes it to you.

This type of event can happen in all the areas of your life: your health, wealth, love and self-expression, but you need to ask if there is a part of you that might resist this change. If so, what are they doing *for* you by stopping you from creating a new experience? Once you understand the reason for the resistance, you can reprogram your mind so that all parts-of-you are working together.

I call the process to make this happen the *Infusion Integration Technique*, which I explain in more detail in Chapter 15.

Chapter 12

The People around You are Parts of You

The people around you represent and demonstrate your inner thoughts and beliefs.

You may have heard about the concept of mirroring. This is when one person subconsciously imitates the gesture, speech pattern, and/or attitude of another.

Mirroring can help establish rapport, since exhibiting similar actions, attitudes, and speech patterns of another person may lead them to believe that you are similar to them and thus more likely to be a friend or a good business associate.

In this discussion of how our thoughts become reality and how we can transform who we are, we are NOT referring to mirroring.

I am suggesting that every person in your life is truly a representative of a part of you. One of your inner sub-personalities is showing up outside of you as a separate person to demonstrate what you are thinking, feeling, and believing.

What if each person in your life in your family, at school, work, or play are the out-picturing and manifestation of your inner thoughts and beliefs?

What if the people around you are representatives of parts-of-you in physical form? What if they are saying and acting out what you are thinking and believing at the deepest level of your psyche?

What if the people around you are actors in your play, performing as characters in your waking dream?

Imagine for a minute that your friends and acquaintances are these representatives of your inner selves showing up as real characters in your life. They are all wearing masks in the form of other faces and names.

These actors have different histories and circumstances that disguise their true identity – the fact that they are a part of you. They have appeared to put on a performance for you that is created by your inner thoughts, concepts, and beliefs.

One person might represent a part of you that you admire. They are those characters who care for you, pay you compliments, and make you feel great. You don't need to change those underlying beliefs. Those sub-personalities are demonstrating that they are healthy and supportive.

Other people in your life may represent parts of you whom you are trying to hide. Maybe these people show up saying things you do not want to hear. They are mean, judgmental, and often upset you with their negative statements that are reminiscent of those voices speaking in your mind.

There may be people who come into your life that even though they may care for you, their words may echo your negative inner voices. You might be trying to block these statements because you don't want to acknowledge what the voices of your sub-personalities are saying inside of you.

The idea of everyone being a part of you can be a frightening thought, and I'm not suggesting that you want negative and difficult people in your life. I'm not saying that you desire people saying things you don't want to hear. But what if their sole purpose was to HELP you see and hear the beliefs you need to change.

What if when you change your inner self,
(your thoughts and beliefs)
you will also change your outer experience?

What if the negative, upsetting, annoying people changed and became more likable? Or if they cannot change, what if those negative people were simply no longer in your life?

We are all intricately connected by energy vibrating in harmony or discord. Through this energetic connection, by changing yourself you change the people around you.

How does this happen? The change begins by your taking the time to evaluate the words that are being said to you. Pay careful attention to the full sentences spoken by the person who is bothering you. You need to reflect on the sentences and conversations that make you angry, fearful, or sad.

Be very aware of statements that "bite" – the words that deeply offend you. Those words may be expressing a belief that a part of you is holding. That belief no longer serves you.

It helps to write the words down on paper. What exactly did that horrible person say?

Examples of statements that may upset you:

Understand that the person is usually saying what you have been thinking or hiding from yourself. Often what they are saying is *true*, but you don't want to hear it. Instead, you begin arguing with them.

Family Member: "You don't spend enough time with your family."
　　You: "I spend time with my family. Look, just two weeks ago we went to Disneyland."
Family Member: "Right, but what about this week and the three months before that?"
　　You: "Oh! That's true. I don't spend much time with my family."

Family Member: "You aren't taking care of your health."
　　You: "I take care of my health. I went for a walk yesterday."
Family Member: "Really? What about the 3 boxes of cookies you ate the day before yesterday? You only get 4 hours of sleep. You don't eat your vegetables."

You: "Oops! True. I'm not taking care of my health."

Partner: "You don't listen to me."

You: "I listen to you. How can I not listen to you?
You are talking all the time."

Partner: "Oh, you mean you listen to me while you watch football or when you are going out the door? You listen to me when you talk on the phone with your friends or text them all day and night."

You: "Got me again. True. I don't listen to him/her."

What do you do about all these true statements you don't want to hear or think about, especially because they were said by someone outside of yourself?

Most often, people become angry and fight the words they don't want to hear. But there is a better way. Look at the truth. Adjust to the truth, and discover what this event is doing **for** you. What is this conversation bringing to your attention? Perhaps you can change the dynamic with friends and family members by changing yourself.

Chapter 13

Becoming "My Angel"

How can we be true to ourselves and others?
By listening carefully to what is being said to you.

One of the many experiences that have proven this concept to me…that our beliefs can be acted out by the people in our lives…is an experience I had with my Mom.

I was in my 40's and had moved in with my Mother when I was recovering from a bad accident. She was working and when she returned to the house in the evening she would be in an angry mood and start yelling at me.

It was extremely upsetting. At first, I defended myself, and then I stopped and became quiet. I remembered the concept that the people outside of me were a part of me, and I decided to use the Infusion Integration Technique to change the dynamic between my mother and me. So, I wrote down exactly what she was saying.

Mom: "You are always on the phone. You don't spend time with the family. You don't talk to me."

Mom continues: "Do you really believe all that stuff you are telling your clients?"

I realized that everything she said was true, and the last statement made me look closely at what I did believe.

I discovered that I did have some doubts about the idea that our thoughts create reality. I realized that those doubts were holding me back. I let myself relax into what I was teaching and learning.

I then asked in my mind (not directly to my Mom), "What if there was a way that I could be on the phone with clients **and** spend time with my family **and** have conversations with Mom more often **and** I could truly believe what I was teaching **and** she would no longer yell at me."

I did the integration, which you will see in the following chapter. (This was done alone, not with her present.)

The next day Mom came home from work and was very nice. During the weeks to come, she started calling me "My Angel", and did so for the rest of her life. I couldn't believe the difference in her. She had completely changed.

Three years later, shortly before she died, I brought up the experience and asked her if she remembered that time when she was always mad at me. Did she realize how much she had changed? (I had *not* told her that I had done the integration technique.)

She looked at me and said, "Yes, I remember that time. I didn't change. You did."

Chapter 14

Is There A Way to Bring All Your Opposing Beliefs Together?

*The Miracle is that the healing power of your Soul
can fit together the pieces of the puzzle together
and your mind can be at peace.*

A major turning point in my life happened in 1977 when I attended a three-day workshop at Sunset Center in Carmel, California, where I was living at the time. The workshop was about a new subject that was being developed at the University of California in Santa Cruse called, "Neurolinguistics Programming". I found it fascinating.

There was one small part of the workshop on the second day when we were told about an integration technique. The leader asked for a volunteer. I raised my hand and was chosen. He asked me to think of a particularly bad time in my life that still bothered me.

I immediately related the time in 1971 when I was Chief Copywriter for an upscale ad agency on Wilshire Boulevard on the "Miracle Mile". It was 5:30 pm in August and I took the elevator down to a small room with two elevators and two doors that led to the underground parking garage. I walked past a man dressed in a guard uniform, and a voice in my mind said, "Run!?" I argued, "Why should I run? It's late. I don't feel like running."

Before I could argue more, the guard had caught me from behind and had his arm around my neck and had a knife at my throat. He was pushing me across the small room as I tried to loosen his stranglehold grip around my neck. Out of nowhere came the words that I said, "Calm down, you're hurting me." (A very strange and obvious statement.)

Suddenly, the elevator door opened in front of me. Three men started to come out. The assailant transferred the knife to my back, stabbed me, pushed me toward the elevator, and ran out the door.

One of the men helped me into the elevator, and my lung collapsed. I slumped to the floor and thought I was dying. When we reached the lobby of the 18-story building, my saviors, who turned out to be lawyers, helped me walk to a desk where I sat and waited for an ambulance. A man who had been in the army in Vietnam held me steady and kept me calm as the police kept asking questions.

When I arrived at the hospital, the nurse punctured my arms many times trying to insert an I.V. Meanwhile, the doctor quickly stabbed me in the chest to insert a tube to inflate my collapsed lung. I was in shock. My world had turned upside down.

Chapter 15

What is the
Infusion Integration Technique?

Six years later, I am in the Neurolinguistics workshop and the leader (I'll call him Greg) began to take me through an integration technique. The process opened the door to healing the deep psychological wound that had been haunting me and keeping me in constant fear for six years.

(This is a more expansive version of the story. It includes all the words that I have added for the Infusion Integration Technique. Greg's version was less descriptive.)

I sat in the front of the room and told Greg and the audience about the stabbing. When I completed my story he asked me to think in terms of having two parts of my being who participated in that event.

He said, "Think of one part of you as a sub-personality who believes the stabbing was a terrible experience. That part is certain that experience should not have happened. Choose one hand to represent that part of you. (I chose my right hand.)

"Now, your other hand will represent a part of you who thinks the stabling did something *for* you.

(I winced at that idea. What did he mean, "It did something *for* me?")

Greg: "Okay, now I am going to ask the one who thinks it would have been better not to be stabbed: "What would have been the advantages of **not** being attacked and stabbed that day?"

I looked at him as if he had two heads. I thought for a few minutes and then the words tumbled out of my mouth:

"Well, of course, I would have been healthy physically and emotionally without that event. I would have stayed on my job, and I would feel safe in garages and elevators. I would be more at ease and sleep better."

"That makes sense," he responded.

"Now tell me the advantages of being stabbed."

"Are you kidding?' I asked.

"No, get into the perspective of that part of you that thinks the stabbing did something for you."

I sat and thought about what could be the advantages.

Finally, I said, "Well my boyfriend, John, had gotten a job and an apartment in San Francisco, and I was still living in L.A. He came back to be with me after I was stabbed."

I see," said Greg. "What else was an advantage?"

I sat quietly for a moment and then said, "I realized this type of event has happened to me before."

"What was that?" he asked.

"I got my feet cut up in a lawnmower when I was twelve, and I now realize that by having that accident, my father stayed with the family another year. I intuitively knew that he was planning to leave for another woman."

"Oh, I see," remarked Gregg. "You sacrificed your well-being to get your father to stay. Instead, of talking to him about it, you became a victim of an accident."

"But I didn't want that to happen," I defended myself.

"Of course not," answered Greg, "but a part of your subconscious came up with that solution."

(This is what the mind can do. Certain beliefs become entrenched in the sub-conscious and then repeat the patterns that match the beliefs. Sometimes we get sick to give us time to relax and contemplate our lives. We keep love out of our lives so we won't be hurt if the person we love goes away. We stop large sums of money from coming to us because it does not fit our version of "reality".)

Greg continued, "Can you think of any other advantages for the stabbing incident in your life?"

"Well, I decided to move back to Carmel where I had gone to high school. I was able to experience a more peaceful life. John joined me and we enjoyed a wonderful lifestyle on the Monterey Peninsula. I became the Director of the Chamber of Commerce and was in TV commercials. That job led to me being Director of Sales at the Lodge at Pebble Beach. None of that would have happened if I had not been stabbed, which prompted me to move back to a place I feel is home."

"So the stabbing set you on a new trajectory," remarked Gregg. "What else?"

"Well, my awareness increased. I pay more attention to the world around me. I listen to my intuition and am gaining trust to follow my guidance immediately. I have been led to many healing workshops, which have helped me, and perhaps I can help others. My intuition brought me to this workshop that has opened my eyes to another world."

"I see," said Greg. "So even though you would prefer that you did not have such a terrible experience, you can see that there were some advantages."

"Yes," I replied reluctantly.

"Now, I would like to ask a question of that part of you who thinks there were advantages to experiencing a traumatic incident in your life.

"What if you could make changes and follow your intuition and guidance and you did not need to experience traumatic, dramatic incidents in your life. What if you pay attention to your heart's desires and can experience the life you choose to live?"

I became quiet and felt the answer, "That would be wonderful," I responded.

"Okay. Please close your eyes and keep your hands apart. I would like to speak to that part of you who in the past thought you needed strong and painful events to wake you up and get your attention. I ask you now to go to the Creative part of your being. You can imagine it as a beautiful room filled with golden light. In the room are computers that provide all the answers in the universe."

Greg continued, "We are asking now for three ways in which Verlaine can listen to and trust her inner guidance and she will no longer need to create difficult physical and/or emotional events to get her attention. She will pay attention to her heart's desires. She will make changes easily and gracefully. She will ask for assistance and speak to those parts of her who have different desires about what they want."

"Verlaine, you do not need to know what those three ways are in consciousness. You will just see yourself acting differently and bringing forth new and wonderful people and experiences.

"Now, please hold your hands up about twelve inches apart with the palms facing each other in front of your chest. Imagine that one hand represents the part of you that did not want to go through a dramatic event. The other hand represents the part of you who could not think of another way to get your attention and thought the advantages would outweigh the problems involved.

"Now, very slowly, bring the two hands (these two parts of you) together until the palms are touching."

I cautiously brought my hands together. There seemed to be some resistance but finally, they were touching.

"Now, entwine the fingers. Imagine the two parts of you hugging each other as you bring your hands up to your heart.

"See all parts of you forming a huddle around the two parts of you. They are sending love and healing to the two in the center. Imagine your Higher Self hovering above this circle of sub-personalities and see your Over-Soul sending love and healing to all parts of your being.

"Imagine now that the two in the center are walking hand-in-hand up a hillside, and they sit down on the grass overlooking a meandering stream and are surrounded by flowering trees and butterflies. The two parts-of-you are talking about how they can work together and how their combined energy will make you stronger.

"Let all parts-of-you know that you are available to discuss problems they are experiencing and that you can do this integration technique to help become whole, complete, and full of energy. And we thank you."

The Infusion Integration Technique
can be used for any area in your life:
Health, Wealth, Love, and Self-Expression.

Instead of a stabbing or accident, you can insert an issue regarding your health (physical, mental, or emotional), lack of wealth, not enough income, no loving relationship, etc.

Using this technique, you can integrate your issues with wealth in terms of receiving an income that provides more money than your needs. You can manifest abundance and a flow of energy in the form of money that helps you maintain all aspects of your life.

You can integrate your interaction with people in terms of experiencing relationships and love and create or maintain relationships with your mate, family, friends, co-workers, etc.

You can discover your unique self-expression. You can integrate those parts of you who would love to use your creative abilities with those sub-personalities who think it is not worth your time.

You can become free of society's limitations. You can identify and allow your creativity and inner expression to flow through you into the world whether it be art and crafts, theater, writing, dance, fashion, interior design or architecture, computer technology, and much, much more.

Why Use the Word "Infusion"?

One morning I asked my Spirit Guides if there should be another name in addition to the *Integration Technique*. At the end of the day, I laid down on my bed and heard the answer to my question. The word I heard in my mind was "Infusion". I looked up the meaning in a dictionary, and one of the definitions was that *Infusion* is a word that describes the moment when "Spirit Enters Form".

I thought, "How perfect!" When we integrate conflicting parts of us and find resolution between opposing belief patterns, we allow our Spirits, our Higher Selves – to enter into our minds and hearts so that we may be guided by our inner knowing and greater awareness.

After many years of using the Infusion Integration Technique with myself and others across the U.S. and in

Japan, Hong Kong, Australia, Bali, and Europe, I have witnessed instantaneous healing and reconciliation.

It appears that the integration helps to dissolve the crystalline belief patterns in the brain and allows the synapses to connect in new ways, thus increasing and releasing energy throughout the body. Individuals can reach a new level of vibrancy.

Your body will come into alignment. Your mind becomes balanced. You are more capable of loving yourself and giving and receiving love from others.

Chapter 16

Using the Infusion Integration Technique

Words and Sequence to heal your mind and heart.
Choosing what's missing is the place to start.

There are many ways to use the *Infusion Integration Technique*. Perhaps you have a problem or a concern about a lack of what you need in the areas of your income, your health, loving relationships, or self-expression, and I would add… you can even integrate those parts of you who are arguing about your spiritual fulfillment. There may be a part of you that says you are not worthy to become the fully operational spiritual being you were meant to be.

The bottom line is if you are not manifesting your heart's desires, begin by asking, "What is missing in my life?"

It may be all of the above, all of the four cornerstones of life: Health, Wealth, Love, and Self-Expression, and your base, Spiritual Fulfilment, however, it is important to start with one area of concern to begin the process.

In this chapter, I explain how to use the Infusion Integration Technique for the concerns about lack of wealth, the absence of abundance and financial security.

Let's say that you would like more wealth in your life. Your outflow is greater than the inflow of money to pay your bills and cover your expenses. You do not have enough money to handle your everyday life, let alone treat yourself to health spas, vacations, a new car, a comfortable home, and all the other benefits of having an abundant supply of money.

Begin by imagining that two parts-of-you hold opposing beliefs regarding wealth:

➢ There is one part-of-you who would like lots of money. Ask that one to choose a hand to represent the "wealth is great" point of view. (It doesn't matter which hand it chooses.)

➢ The other part of you thinks it is **best not** to have too much money. Ask that one to use the other hand to represent the "less is better" point of view.

Greet each of them as if they are separate beings. (These are not considered male or female parts of you. They are sub-personalities who are the *keepers of your beliefs*, and it is their job to gather proof that their beliefs are true.)

➢ Now ask the one who would like lots of money, **"What are the advantages of being rich?"**

Some of the answers might be:

- I can buy new clothes and find a new place to live.
- I can go on an extended vacation and visit places I have always wanted to see.
- I can help my family, friends, and other people.
- I can change jobs and perhaps work independently.
- I can buy lots of presents
- I can live in a big, lovely house

Now ask your other sub-personality represented by the other hand, "What are the advantages of **not** being rich?"

Normally, the one who wants to be rich will try to interrupt and say there are no advantages to **not** being rich.

You respond with, "Thank you for sharing, but you need to be quiet now. I need answers to this question from the one who is stopping me from being wealthy. Because if that part wasn't there, I would be rich! Please let that part of me talk."

It may take a few minutes for the "Less is Better" part of you to respond. They may ask again, "Advantages of *not* being rich? You mean the advantages of being poor?"

- "Yes, that is the question."
- "Well, I guess I won't need to pay a lot of taxes."
- "Okay, we'll put that on the list. What else?"

Make another column on your paper for the answers about the advantages of not being rich. Some answers might be:

What are the advantages of **NOT** being rich?

- My friends will not be jealous of me.
- I can be more spiritual.
- I can be free of responsibility.
- I can do what I want.
- I don't have to worry about how to invest my money.
- No one will want to take my money away.

Add as many answers to your list as you can think of regarding it is better not to be rich. Always list the opposition in terms of advantages.

After completing your two lists, ask the "Best not to be rich" part of you this question: "If there were a way that you could be wealthy, **AND you could**

- buy new clothes and live in a place that you love and that you can afford,
- you could go on vacation to places you have always wanted to see and have fun,
- you could help your family and other people,
- and you could change jobs if you wanted to and perhaps work independently.

AND

- your friends wouldn't be jealous of you,
- you could still be spiritual and a good person,
- you could still feel free of responsibility by having people help you do your tasks,
- and you could do what you want,
- you could collect a bunch of stuff or not.
- you wouldn't have to invest your money. You could just leave it in the bank or learn about investing,
- no one would try to take your money away.
- and people would love you for yourself.

If you could have the advantages of being rich AND the advantages of not being rich, would you be willing to change your behavior and let this person become wealthy and enjoy the benefits of being rich?

Sometimes, the part of you that was holding you back, i.e. keeping your poor, sick, with no one to love, etc. will hesitate to answer. You can ask, is there something more you would need so that you would change your behavior and let this person become wealthier?"

They might answer something like, "Well, I wouldn't want to act crazy if I were rich."

The answer: "Okay, you will be sane and logical about your wealth. All of your best qualities will just become better."

"Okay.

Observer: "Good.

Now, I ask you to close your eyes and ask that part of you who was restricting the flow of money to go to the Creative Part of Your Being.

Imagine this to be a beautiful room filled with golden light. There are angelic beings present as well as magical computers that know all the answers of the Universe.

We're going to ask for three ways that you can receive money and maintain all of the advantages of being poor and receive all the advantages of being wealthy.

We ask that all parts of you check those three ways and make sure that they are a win/win for all parts of you.

You do not need to know what those three ways are in consciousness at this time. You will simply feel and act differently as you begin to receive the wealth you deserve.

Now I would like you to hold your two hands up with the palms facing each other.

See the part-of-you on one hand who wanted to protect you by stopping the flow of energy in the form of money.

See the other part-of-you who would love to use wealth for good purposes.

Now, slowly bring the two hands together until they are touching.

Entwine the fingers and bring your two hands up to your heart.

Imagine all parts of you forming a circle around the two parts-of-you and sending them love and healing.

See your Higher Self sending love and healing to the two in the center of the circle.

Now see the two parts walking hand in hand and up onto a grass-covered hillside. Flowering trees are growing next to a stream and butterflies floating on the breeze.

The two parts-of-you discuss how they are going to work together to help you receive money and build the wealth you desire.

We thank these two for communicating in consciousness and let all parts-of-you know that you are available to listen and help to bring them together to operate as a powerful whole person in the world.

And we thank you.

More information with examples regarding the Infusion Integration Technique are available in my book, "Ending the Battle Within", which is available on Amazon, or the book can be ordered directly from me at www.verlainecrawford.com.

Chapter 17

Cosmic Bridges
and the Desires of Your Heart

So many pathways to follow each day
so many choices along the way.

You may notice something different about yourself as the days go by. You might feel a change has happened. You seem to have more energy. You smile more easily. There appears to be a new brightness about you. You also notice that you are meeting new people, entertaining new ideas, and making plans that would normally be more difficult for you.

Something has changed but you don't know why or when it happened.

As time passes, life becomes easier. You are no longer in conflict with others or with your interior self. It is as if you have become an alternative self. And then you remember.

It was a dream, or at least it seemed like a dream. It appeared to be early morning or was it late afternoon? A cool mist was blowing across a lonely, tree-lined road. You found yourself walking up a gentle slope toward an unknown destination. But for some reason, you felt you were not alone.

Someone was walking just ahead of you at a slightly faster pace. You also sensed a presence behind you and turned to see a shadowy figure following you.

You found yourself between two unknown figures. The shadowy figure behind you seemed very familiar. And the one moving quickly ahead was compelling as if it possessed a magnetic quality of being.

More of the dream floats into your mind. You see a bridge that possesses an unusual illumination. You watch intently as the figure ahead of you crosses over the long and narrow bridge and stands to wait for you on the other side. As you approach the entrance to the bridge, you turn around to see the familiar figure behind you beckoning you to return.

Somewhere deep inside you know you have reached a tipping point. A decision has to be made. It is a point of critical departure…seeking the unknown or returning to what is safe and familiar. You take a deep breath. The fear that you have been holding deep inside seems to fade away. Something is compelling you forward, and you begin to cross the bridge.

The bridge is glowing. It seems to be illuminated from its inner structure soaring high above the valley below. You can hear soft and gentle laughter as you approach the end of the bridge. You feel lighter. The stranger is waiting for you.

For some reason, there is no fear. When only a few feet away, you begin to see the being more clearly and distinctly, smiling directly at you.

As you approach, you recognize the smile. It is your smile, only brighter. Those are your eyes, only clearer. The figure appears to be taller, straighter, and possesses more energy than you. And then, you realize it is you. Suddenly, the figure disappears, and you awaken from the dream. But was it only a dream?

In each of our lives, there are moment points – critical points of departure. We need to recognize these cosmic bridges when we are beckoned to cross. Many of us find ourselves caught within the struggle of two worlds – the world of our past and the world of our future. The question is: Which world? Which you?

For you to become your highest self and utilize the power of the magnetic fields that you possess, you need to release the restrictions of your past. You need to leave behind the shadowy beliefs that you once perceived as the absolute rulers of your life.

Look anew at what is true for you. Which beliefs do you choose to guide your thoughts and actions? You can change your underlying beliefs…the seeds of manifestation.

Isn't it time for you to manifest what you desire while utilizing your talents and abilities? Wouldn't it be wonderful if your activities delighted and empowered you?

It is time to decide to lighten your load and move forward with enthusiasm and energy. You are on your way toward your ultimate destiny.

Chapter 18

Moment Points, Magnetic Fields and Manifestation

When reviewing the process of creating your life,
you can choose methods that will reduce strife
and thus increase your magnetic field,
so you can relax, receive, and be healed.

Reduce Pride and Prejudice

It is easy for us to put up walls and barriers by pre-judging and applying prideful limitations on what we believe is our reality. By eliminating the walls, we leave the door open to new probabilities that can include meaningful adventures and exciting opportunities.

Release Your Expectations

Most of us possess pre-conceived expectations derived from experiences from our past. We project these expectations into our future. By releasing these projections we can open to the unknown, which can be far greater than we imagined.

Open Your Heart

Your heart is the center of your magnetic field, which is 5000 times greater than the brain. People often define themselves through a mind interpretation of who they think they should be. The true definition of self emanates from the heart. It is from this central, harmonic, pulse point that we magnetize what fits our true identity.

Expect the Unexpected

The world wants us to believe that A + B = C. In the world of magnetic fields and manifestation, there is no A + B. We need to be aware of *indicators, signs, and confirmations* that may lead us to discover new, unexpected gateways to enter into life-changing events.

Listen Beyond Judgments

It is important to reach a new level of awareness in listening and interpreting our world. Far too much information passes by us daily that could provide pertinent guidance for future events. Our minds are wonderful censors that automatically eliminate anything that is not deemed necessary or essential. It is critical to listen beyond the judgments of our minds.

Own Your Deservedness

Know that you are worthy and deserve to receive. When you are vibrating from your Heart, you are extending and accepting Love from the Center of Your Being. Once you have created a vibrating, magnetic core, it will encircle you and serve as a broadcasting beacon.

Stand In the Center of the Magnetic Field and Allow It to Encircle You

Your heart is the harmonic, magnetic center of attraction that works effortlessly and continuously to match your needs and desires. You will attract and manifest with the power of Love. This process requires no reasoning or mind intervention.

Relax and Let Go

When you understand the seven principal steps above, you can relax and let go. There is nothing else you need to do to manifest your desires.

Expect Joy in Your Receivership

The emotion and satisfaction from receiving the manifested desires of your heart should be celebrated and lived as a joyful experience. This expectation of joy helps to intensify the magnetic field.

Practice Gratefulness and Thanksgiving

By acknowledging your heart-felt desires as already received, you set up a vibration for the future event to manifest. Allow your words and thoughts to live within the aura of your being. Live in gratitude for what you have and what you will receive.

Acknowledge the Process
of Magnetic Manifestation

Know and realize that this process has been used by some of the most important figures in our world history – many that you already know, such as Leonardo da Vinci, Albert Einstein, Jonas Salk, Nikola Tesla, and Madame Curie, artists, scientists, sports figures, business people, and many more.

Realize that there are many moment points in our lives when we come upon cosmic bridges to cross. We can be prepared to accept these opportunities, or we can turn away in fear. You have been given the freedom of choice, and you now possess the understanding of the process. It is up to you to become your progressed, future self, or to remain hidden and cloaked within the safe confines of your past.

May your guidance lead you to wonderful experiences for your very best health, wealth, love, self-expression, and your awakening to all you can be!

A Note from Verlaine

I hope you enjoyed "The Heart of Transformation and The Butterfly Effect". I plan to write more books that delve into all aspects of healing your heart and soul in the near future.

In the meantime, I am available to serve as a mentor, teacher, and resource for those who wish to embark and/or continue on their journey to wholeness. There are so many aspects of you, so many facets emblazoned into the diamond of your infinite, multidimensional soul. I would love to share with you what I have learned and teach you how to apply this information in your life.

If there is a group or organization you would like me to speak to or you would like a one-on-one consultation on Zoom or Skype, please let me know. I have also presented seminars, workshops, and retreats to corporate groups, as well as counselors, coaches, and trainers. I look forward to hearing from you.

Verlaine

VerlaineCrawford@gmail.com

About the Author

Verlaine Crawford enjoyed her formative years in Iowa by the Mississippi River with 40 acres of forest in her back yard. She learned the wonder of nature and gained the ability to meditate under the spreading oaks and pine trees.

Verlaine went to high school in Carmel, California, and studied International Relations at the University of California at Berkeley. She learned marketing on the job in ad agencies in Los Angeles, eventually forming Crawford Marketing Consultants, which worked with many types of businesses from architecture to health care, hospitality to high tech, including co-founding two software companies in Silicon Valley. She was CEO of three Chambers of Commerce and Director of Corporate Fundraising for the AIDS Services Foundation.

In the 1990s, she was invited to travel to Japan, Hong Kong, Australia, and Europe teaching the Infusion Integration Technique to students and counselors.

Verlaine has been a consultant to celebrities, executives, entrepreneurs, and Fortune 500 companies. She has studied, tested, and used her knowledge of Metaphysics to achieve business success. She has enjoyed a 50-year, loving relationship, great health, exciting creative expression; and best of all, her inner work has given her the gift of a peaceful mind.

Order Books by Verlaine Crawford

by contacting her at
VerlaineCrawford@gmail.com
www.VerlaineCrawford.com

"Ending the Battle Within:
How to Create a Harmonious Life by Working
with Your Sub-Personalities"

"Daughter of God:
Angelic Messages of Wisdom and Love"

Edited and Published by Verlaine:

"Portals in Time: The Quest for Un-Old-Age"
by John Joseph Teressi
www.JohnTeressi.com

"The Alchemy of the Seven Harmonies:
Empower, Energize, Expand"
by John Joseph Teressi

Available on Amazon and Barnes & Noble

www.ingramcontent.com/pod-product-compliance
Lightning Source LLC
Chambersburg PA
CBHW031416040426
42444CB00005B/598